GUIDELI

MW01064580

Small Group
Ministries

*Christian
Formation Through
Mutual Accountability*

Steven W. Manskar
The General Board of Discipleship

SMALL GROUP MINISTRIES

Copyright © 2012 by Cokesbury

This book is printed on acid-free paper.

ISBN 978-1-426-73633-9

Some paragraph numbers for and language in the Book of Discipline *may have changed in the 2012 revision, which was published after these Guidelines were printed. We regret any inconvenience.*

MANUFACTURED IN THE UNITED STATES OF AMERICA

Contents

Called to a Ministry of Faithfulness and Vitality

You are so important to the life of the Christian church! You have consented to join with other people of faith who, through the millennia, have sustained the church by extending God's love to others. You have been called and have committed your unique passions, gifts, and abilities to a position of leadership. This Guideline will help you understand the basic elements of that ministry within your own church and within The United Methodist Church.

Leadership in Vital Ministry

Each person is called to ministry by virtue of his or her baptism, and that ministry takes place in all aspects of daily life, both in and outside of the church. Your leadership role requires that you will be a faithful participant in the **mission of the church**, which is to partner with God to **make disciples of Jesus Christ for the transformation of the world.** You will not only engage in your area of ministry, but will also work to empower others to be in ministry as well. The vitality of your church, and the Church as a whole, depends upon the faith, abilities, and actions of all who work together for the glory of God.

Clearly then, as a pastoral leader or leader among the laity, your ministry is not just a "job," but a spiritual endeavor. You are a spiritual leader now, and others will look to you for spiritual leadership. What does this mean?

All persons who follow Jesus are called to grow spiritually through the practice of various Christian habits (or "means of grace") such as prayer, Bible study, private and corporate worship, acts of service, Christian conferencing, and so on. Jesus taught his disciples practices of spiritual growth and leadership that you will model as you guide others. As members of the congregation grow through the means of grace, they will assume their own role in ministry and help others in the same way. This is the cycle of disciple making.

The Church's Vision

While there is one mission—to make disciples of Jesus Christ—the portrait of a successful mission will differ from one congregation to the next. One of your roles is to listen deeply for the guidance and call of God in your own context. In your church, neighborhood, or greater community, what are the greatest needs? How is God calling your congregation to be in a ministry of service and witness where they are? What does vital ministry look like in the life of your congregation and its neighbors? What are the characteristics, traits, and actions that identify a person as a faithful disciple in your context?

This portrait, or vision, is formed when you and the other leaders discern together how your gifts from God come together to fulfill the will of God.

Assessing Your Efforts

We are generally good at deciding what to do, but we sometimes skip the more important first question of what we want to accomplish. Knowing your task (the mission of disciple making) and knowing what results you want (the vision of your church) are the first two steps in a vital ministry. The third step is in knowing how you will assess or measure the results of what you do and who you are (and become) because of what you do. Those measures relate directly to mission and vision, and they are more than just numbers.

One of your leadership tasks will be to take a hard look, with your team, at all the things your ministry area does or plans to do. No doubt they are good and worthy activities; the question is, *"Do these activities and experiences lead people into a mature relationship with God and a life of deeper discipleship?"* That is the business of the church, and the church needs to do what only the church can do. You may need to eliminate or alter some of what you do if it does not measure up to the standard of faithful disciple making. It will be up to your ministry team to establish the specific standards against which you compare all that you do and hope to do. (This Guideline includes further help in establishing goals, strategies, and measures for this area of ministry.)

The Mission of The United Methodist Church

Each local church is unique, yet it is a part of a *connection*, a living organism of the body of Christ. Being a connectional Church means in part that all United Methodist churches are interrelated through the structure and organization of districts, conferences, and jurisdictions in the larger "family" of the denomination. *The Book of Discipline of The United Methodist Church* describes, among other things, the ministry of all United Methodist Christians, the essence of servant ministry and leadership, how to organize and accomplish that ministry, and how our connectional structure works (see especially ¶¶126–138).

Our Church extends way beyond your doorstep; it is a global Church with both local and international presence. You are not alone. The resources of the entire denomination are intended to assist you in ministry. With this help and the partnership of God and one another, the mission continues. You are an integral part of God's church and God's plan!

(For help in addition to this Guideline and the *Book of Discipline*, see "Resources" at the end of your Guideline, www.umc.org, and the other websites listed on the inside back cover.)

Ministry and Small Groups

W hy are small groups important? Why did John Wesley place so much confidence in them as a dependable means of grace for developing faith and holiness? The answers to these questions begin with the Trinity: God as Father, Son, and Holy Spirit.

This is important because human beings are created in the image of God (Genesis 1:26a, 27). The "image of God" means that human character is a reflection of God's character. We are not exact replicas of God, but we are representations or likenesses of God. This means that human beings are, like the Triune God, relational creatures. God created us with the capacity to give and receive love. We are made for relationship with God, with one another, and with creation.

God's nature is revealed in the relationships within the Trinity: the Father loves the Son; the Son loves the Father; the Father and Son love the Holy Spirit. Each person is unique in character and work. At the same time each person participates in the life and work of the others.

An excellent illustration of the relational nature of the image of God and its importance to human lives and communities is the southern African concept known as *ubuntu* that teaches: *I am because we are.* It means that I can only become fully me as long I am in relationship with you. *Ubuntu* is rooted in the belief that all people are created in the image of God and that fact determines our value, meaning, and potential. To be fully human, therefore, is to be part of a community of love and forgiveness. *Ubuntu* tells us that we cannot be fully human apart from community. We become fully the persons God created us to be only within the relationships made possible in community. Our relationship with God is shaped by our relationships with others whom God loves.

When Christians meet in small groups to pray, to study Scripture, to be in fellowship, and to serve they find Christ in one another because they form relationships of love and trust. Certainly Sunday morning worship and general congregational activities play an essential role, but on their own they are not adequate substitutes for the relationships formed in small groups. This is why gathering together in small groups is essential to the church's mission of making disciples of Jesus Christ for the transformation of the world.

Today, we may describe small groups as gatherings of 3 to 15 people who meet regularly (weekly, bi-weekly, or monthly) to help one another grow in holiness of heart and life and to help the congregation participate in God's

mission in the world. Group members attend to the ways that God is at work
in their lives and do all in their power to cooperate with God's grace. The
group meets to watch over one another in love. They support and encourage
one another in the practice of missional and incarnational discipleship.

Holiness

Holiness of heart (loving God with your whole being) and life (loving
neighbor as oneself) is the goal of discipleship (Matthew 22:37-40).
Holiness is a life shaped by the love described by Paul in 1 Corinthians
13:1-13 and by Jesus in John 15:12-17. It is the way of discipleship Jesus
describes in Luke 9:23. John Wesley frequently described holiness as "having the mind of Christ" (Philippians 2:5).

Growth in holiness requires a community that is organized to help its members keep the promises made in the Baptismal Covenant: To proclaim the
good news and live according to the example of Christ; to surround these
persons with a community of love and forgiveness, that they may grow in
their trust of God, and be found faithful in their service to others; and to
pray for them, that they may be true disciples who walk in the way that
leads to life (See page 35 in *The United Methodist Hymnal*).

In the *Commendation and Welcome* the congregation is enjoined to "Do all
in your power to increase their faith, confirm their hope, and perfect them in
love." This means congregations must order their life in ways that cooperate
with the dynamic of grace that is prevenient, justifying, and sanctifying.

Missional

When a congregation is intentional about forming members into disciples of
Jesus Christ by living the Baptismal Covenant, it becomes a Christ-centered
outpost of the reign of God. An outpost is like an embassy that represents a
nation in a foreign land. In like manner, missional congregations represent
the reign of God in the world.

Congregations become missional when they systematically equip and send
members to participate with Christ in God's mission, which is the intentional restoration of *shalom* for all of Creation. *Shalom* describes a world in
which justice, righteousness, and lovingkindness are the norm. It is a world
in which all people have all they need to live and thrive; to become fully the
persons God created them to be. *Shalom* is what Christians pray for when
they say: "Your kingdom come, on earth as it is in heaven."

Missional congregations center their resources and order their life in ways
that equip members to be witnesses and practioners of *shalom* in the world.

They understand that personal and social holiness are two sides of the same coin. One cannot be genuine without the other. The fruit of holiness is a people who are engaged both in works of piety (loving God) and works of mercy (loving neighbor).

Wesley taught that the works of piety must be balanced by the works of mercy. Feeding the hungry, clothing the naked, sheltering the homeless, visiting the sick and imprisoned, and welcoming strangers are how Christians historically love their neighbor as themselves (Mark 12:31; Matthew 25:31-46). Wesley urged Methodists to be people who love God with all they are and have. And, because they love God, Methodists love those whom God loves, as God loves them.

Contextual

Historically, the Methodist small group system was pastoral and contextual. This means that it emerged from the pastoral commitment to do all in one's power to increase faith, confirm hope in Christ, and perfect one another in love. Wesley did not find the system in a book or a program. It emerged from the needs of the people and his openness to trying new ideas. The groups described on pages 12-13 are the result of ideas that worked. There were other attempts at groups that didn't contribute to the Methodist mission and were discontinued. This means the system that will work best for your people will not come from a "one-size-fits-all" program. It will emerge from the pastoral ministry of the congregation and will fit your local context. The questions to ask as you evaluate are:
1. How does this system/group help this congregation experience and demonstrate God's grace?
2. How does the system/group help persons to grow in holiness of heart and life? and
3. How does the system/group equip the people to participate in Christ's mission in the world?

The Wesleyan tradition teaches us that several types of groups are essential. We need groups that initiate seekers into Christian faith and life. Other groups promote continuing growth in faith, hope, and love through support and accountability. Others support those engaged in service and justice. Finally, persons who provide leadership at all levels need a group for training and nurture.

A Biblical/Theological Foundation

through the Sacrament of Baptism we are initiated into Christ's holy church. We are incorporated into God's mighty acts of salvation and given new birth through water and the Spirit. All this is God's gift, offered to us without price" (Baptismal Covenant; *Hymnal*, page 33).

"Therefore, ... work out your own salvation with fear and trembling; for it is God who is at work in you, enabling you both to will and to work for his good pleasure" (Philippians 2:12-13).

The Baptismal Covenant tells us that salvation and our place in the church are gifts from God. They are freely given because God made us. There is nothing you or I could ever do or say to earn or deserve these gifts. God gives them because "God is love" (see 1 John 4:7-21). The word that best describes God's love is "grace."

Understanding Grace

Grace is the presence and power of God working in the world, and it is unlimited and free. Jesus Christ is grace embodied in human flesh and blood. His life, death, and resurrection reveal the nature and power of grace as God's love active in, with, and for the world. Through him God enters human life and history saying: "Come to me, all you that are weary and are carrying heavy burdens, and I will give you rest. Take my yoke upon you, and learn from me; for I am gentle and humble in heart, and you will find rest for your souls. For my yoke is easy, and my burden is light" (Matthew 11:28-30).

Preventing (also known as prevenient) grace prepares us to accept God's acceptance and love. Justifying grace restores our relationship with God and those whom God loves by giving us the gifts of repentance and faith (outward, relational change). Sanctifying grace gives new birth and sustains us in the new life of holiness with Jesus in the world (inward, real change). All this is to say that God supplies the grace we need to accept the gift of his love and then to live as a channel of that love in the world. When we live the way of Jesus we become fully the persons God created us to be, in the image of Christ.

THE MEANS OF GRACE

As we consider the "why" and "how" of small group ministry, we begin with Jesus' promise: "For where two or three are gathered in my name, I am there among them" (Matthew 18:20). It's because of Jesus' promise that

John Wesley believed small groups to be a "means of grace":

> By 'means of grace' I understand outward signs, words, or actions
> ordained of God, and appointed for this end—to be the ordinary channels
> whereby he might convey to men preventing, justifying, or sanctifying
> grace (see Sermon 16: "The Means of Grace" in *John Wesley's Sermons*,
> edited by Outler and Heitzenrater, or another anthology of Wesley's ser-
> mons).

When two or more Christians regularly meet in Jesus' name to pray, sing,
study, serve, and watch over one another in love, grace opens their hearts to
God. Small groups are where people get the support and accountability they
need to follow Jesus in the world. Through relationships of love and trust
they learn the Christian spiritual practices that change the habits and attitudes that are blockages to grace so that grace can flow through them for the
world. Wesley also called these habits and attitudes "holy tempers." The
Apostle Paul called them "fruit of the Spirit": ... love, joy, peace, patience,
kindness, generosity, faithfulness, gentleness, and self-control (Galatians
5:22-23). (To learn more read Wesley's Sermon 43: "The Scripture Way of
Salvation.")

In the sacrament of baptism, the pastor instructs the congregation to accept
responsibility for the ongoing Christian formation of their new sisters and
brothers in Christ by "doing all in their power" to see that all members
receive the help they need to grow in holiness of heart and life. We see here
that baptism marks the beginning of a life-long process, a pilgrimage. The
destination is holiness of heart and life; also known as perfection in love.

The mutual support and accountability experienced in small groups are how
the church keeps the promises it makes in the Baptismal Covenant. In small
groups Christians receive the support they need to "work out their salvation." They open themselves to grace so that God can work in them to instill
in them habits and attitudes that are reflections of "the mind of Christ Jesus"
(Philippians 2:5). They gain guidance in how to extend themselves in love
to their neighbor, in the community, nation, and world.

BELIEVING, BEHAVING, BELONGING

Wesley clearly understood that Christian formation (disciple making) does
not happen by accident, but by intention and with discipline. Discipline, for
Wesley, is simply a habitual practice of the means of grace (or Christian
spiritual disciplines, known as "works of piety" and "walks of mercy") supported by weekly accountability in a small group. He knew that Christians
are formed by initiating persons into a new way of behavior shaped by the

teachings of Jesus Christ. Christian discipline is summarized by three words: believing, behaving, and belonging.

Beliefs are enacted in behavior. John Wesley understood that people are much more likely to behave their way into believing than they are to believe their way into behaving as a Christian. That is why he required all Methodists to participate in the weekly Class Meeting. He taught them the means of grace—doing no harm by avoiding evil, doing good to all people as often as possible, prayer, reading and studying Scripture, public worship, the Lord's Supper, and fasting or abstinence. These are the behaviors that equip Christians to deny themselves, take up their cross daily, and follow Jesus (Luke 9:23).

United Methodist Beliefs
The beliefs (or essential doctrines) of Christian faith for United Methodists are contained in the Articles of Religion, Confession of Faith, (found in Part II: Doctrinal Standards and Our Theological Task of the *Book of Discipline*) and the standard sermons of John Wesley (Sermons #1-52). Congregations must assure that all members know and grasp these essential teachings. The beliefs contained in these doctrines are enacted by the congregation in the rituals of baptism and the Lord's Supper. They are summarized when the congregation recites the Nicene and Apostles' creeds in worship (*Hymnal* #880-882).

Learning and practicing the means of grace is how most Methodists came to believe and receive the gift of faith. They behaved their way into believing. Behaving and believing are a part of belonging in Christian community. The practices of Christian belief and behavior define the character of Christian community described in the Baptismal Covenant as being a "community of love and forgiveness" that forms people as "disciples who walk in the way that leads to life."

Behave, believe, and belong are all entry points into the way of Jesus. They are inter-related parts of the process of disciple formation that builds upon the relational nature of human beings. "You become what you love." If the goal of Christian formation is for persons to become more and more like Christ, then we need to know him as a living Savior. Congregations make disciples of Jesus Christ when they offer safe places for people to explore Christian beliefs, practices, and community.

A Historical Foundation

i n the Wesleyan Methodist tradition Christian formation happens in an integrated system of small groups that enables the congregation to receive and participate in the grace that forms persons as disciples of Jesus Christ.

In this prayer excerpt Wesley summarizes the *dynamic of grace* as the work of prevenient, justifying, and sanctifying grace (see also page 9) that works in the lives and hearts of individuals and congregations in the world: "O that we may all receive of Christ's fullness, grace upon grace; grace to pardon our sins, and subdue our iniquities; to justify our persons and to sanctify our souls; and to complete that holy change, that renewal of our hearts, whereby we may be transformed into that blessed image wherein thou didst create us." (See "A collection of Prayers for Families—Friday Morning," *The Works of Wesley*, Vol. 11: 254.)

A Wesleyan Model

A good example of a system of small groups designed to cooperate with the dynamic of grace is found in the early Methodist societies. John Wesley and the early Methodists developed a system of groups, each with a different theological/pastoral emphasis. The system met people where they were and helped them to grow and mature in holiness of heart and life. The Wesleyan system was composed of three distinctive types of groups:
1. The Class Meeting (*for everyone*)
2. The Band (*for the deeply committed disciples*)
3. The Select Society (*for the leaders*)

THE CLASS MEETING
When a person joined a Methodist society he or she was assigned to a "class," a small group of 12-15 women and men. Participation in a class was compulsory for all Methodists. Each class was lead by a society member. Class leaders were lay persons who demonstrated Christian maturity and pastoral sense. All of the class leaders were lay men and women.

Classes met weekly, either in the leader's home or in the local Methodist meeting house. Meetings were typically an hour and consisted of prayer, hymn singing, Scripture reading and study, and accountability for discipleship. The class meeting initiated Methodists into the life of discipleship. The focus was on teaching the basics of Christian faith and life and helping members to live in the world as faithful followers of Jesus. The theological emphases were prevenient and convincing grace; that is, recognizing that

God invites, woos, cajoles, and leads us to accept his acceptance of us in Jesus Christ and adoption as a beloved child in God's household.

THE BAND
The "band" was for Methodists who faithfully attended their class meeting and were ready to go deeper in holiness. Membership was limited to no more than eight men or women. Bands were organized according to gender and marital status because of the nature of the group: single men together, single women in a different band, and so on.

Bands met weekly for one hour with shared leadership. The weekly agenda included opening with prayer and singing, Scripture reading, and conversation that included confession of sins to one another.

The theological emphasis of the band meeting was justification and justifying grace; that is, making a decision, with God's help, toward repentance and a changed life in faith. The group was a safe place to confess sins to peers. They encouraged a depth of sharing and support through prayer and encouragement that the class meeting was not designed to provide. Members grew in holiness through the relationships of mutual love and trust.

THE SELECT SOCIETY
Disciple-making congregations need leaders; lay women and men who are seasoned disciples of Jesus Christ who habitually engage in prayer, study, and service and are earnestly striving after holiness of heart and life. They are the disciples who make disciples and who lead the congregation in its service with Christ in the world. In early Methodism, all members of the Select Society served in some leadership role in the society and also in their parish church.

The theological emphasis of the Select Society was sanctification; that is, with God's help, devoting themselves to loving God with all their heart, soul, and mind. They loved their neighbors as themselves and they loved one another as Christ loved them. They knew that the world would know they were disciples of Jesus Christ by the way they loved one another (see John 13:34-35).

A Contemporary Model

We recognize that Methodist societies were not churches, but religious communities of high expectations and loving discipline. That is why participation in a small group was required for all Methodists. Obviously, 18th-century Methodist societies were very different from today's congregations, so we should not try to replicate that system. Nevertheless, Wesley's theological and practical understanding of Christian formation is both valid and timeless and provides essential guidance.

1. Making disciples requires a community that cooperates with the work of grace and the Holy Spirit.
2. Making disciples happens most effectively through the relationships formed in small groups.
3. Disciple-making congregations develop an integrated system of small groups that meet people where they are and help them grow in holiness of heart and life.

This Guideline is not about a one-size-fits-all small group program. You will find here a guide for developing a ministry that fits your local context and culture. We know from the Wesleyan tradition that developing and sustaining small group ministry is a process of trial and error. When an idea falls flat, learn from it and try again. Eventually you will find the system that works best for your context. This, of course, assumes that the work is guided by prayer, worship, openness to grace, and the leading of the Holy Spirit.

Grace Groups

Every congregation has small groups but they may not be considered to be "small groups." They are more commonly known as the church council, the pastor/staff-parish relations committee, the trustees, the finance committee, the choir, Sunday school classes, and so on, and all can be places of faith formation and discipleship. Disciple-making congregations plan for all groups to be places where relationships of love, support, and accountability are formed and members grow in holiness of heart and life. We describe these as *Grace Groups*.

Examine the existing groups in your congregation and determine where they fit in a system of "grace groups," described more fully in the sample below. *Though these are presented in a linear structure, they are not so tidy, and they overlap.* The goal is to organize the groups to help the congregation cooperate with God's prevenient, justifying, and sanctifying grace; remembering that different activities and experiences may fit in more than one place. Within this system, lives are transformed as people learn and engage in Christian spiritual practices and order their lives in new ways. *This chart is suggestive, and you will want to order it in a way that makes sense in your context.* (See Resources for more information about these types of groups.)

Grace Groups I *Preventing and Convincing Grace*	Grace Groups II *Justifying and Sanctifying Grace*	Grace Groups III *Sanctifying Grace*
Class Meeting	Covenant Discipleship groups	Covenant Discipleship groups
New Member classes	Emmaus Reunion groups	Emmaus Reunion
Wesley Fellowship Groups	Life Transformation Groups (LTG)	Academy of Spiritual Formation covenant groups
Life Transformation Groups (LTG)	Renovaré groups	Accountability groups
Bible Study groups		Leadership groups
Prayer groups		Life Transformation Groups (LTG)
Book study groups		Administrative & Ministry Committees
Companions in Christ		
Choirs		

GRACE GROUP I

Some Grace Groups are needed for new Christians, or people seeking to become Christians. These people may be new to the church, new to United Methodism, and/or new to Christianity. Such groups are lead by mature disciples. Their mission is to teach the basic practices and beliefs of Christian faith and life. These entry level groups emphasize Christian teaching, formation, and "watching over one another in love" guided by the General Rules.

Remember that some new Christians come because they are curious, but open, to the faith. They have questions about finding and making meaning, about God or Jesus, about the observance of the Christian seasons, or other theologically-based inquiries. Others enter through participation in service and then learn more about the theological basis for their service (behaving, then believing). All groups can be places of faith formation and disciple making, whether they are oriented first to spiritual growth or to a ministry or task. Some of the groups listed on the chart are mainly intended for personal and community spiritual enrichment; others include a dimension of service beyond the church.

GRACE GROUP II

As people grow in faith and begin to mature in holiness through support and accountability, they will reach a point where they need a group that nurtures continued growth as they attune themselves more closely to hearing and doing what they perceive is God's will for them.

Congregations need to provide groups that help people who are ready to go deeper in loving God and neighbors. The theological emphasis in such groups will be justifying grace. This means that they will emphasize the development of relationships shaped by trust and personal story sharing, even confession. Such groups help the congregation to keep its baptismal promise to nurture others in a community of love and forgiveness that engenders trust of God and urges service to others (see Baptismal Covenant I, section 8).

The only agenda for Grace Groups II is discipleship—taking action within and outside the church as God calls. At this stage, people will be ready to take responsibility for their own spiritual growth and for acting on their faith in the world. They will need to receive and offer accountability and support.

GRACE GROUP III

Grace Groups III are for *leaders* in discipleship. Their focus is upon "earnestly striving after perfection in love." These groups are for those who have experienced justification by grace through faith and desire Christian maturity. The focus of these groups is the entire love of God and neighbor, which means that through the practice of various spiritual disciplines, they are actively seeking to learn God's will and direction for them and then to follow, even if that response places them at odds with the norms or values of our society and culture. These leaders need to be equipped, empowered, and supported in their ministry.

The examples of groups here include those that have a deeper dimension of Christian formation, but the administrative and ministry groups are suggested here as well. Ideally, each of the ministry groups in your church tends not simply to the tasks for which they are responsible, but also takes care to shape and form the people in those groups as deeply committed Christians. These group members not only follow God's call in all aspects of their lives, they also identify the gifts in others and cultivate them in faith and leadership.

Getting Started

S mall group ministry is not a program. It is how the church forms people as disciples and nurtures them towards holiness of heart and life. Every church has small groups in some kind of system (though it may not be intentional or systematic). The system must reflect the personalities and needs of the people and the place.

The easiest way to begin with small group ministry is to build upon existing groups. If the congregation is making disciples of Jesus Christ for the transformation of the world, then all the administrative and ministry committees can, and even must, be places of Christian formation.

The following are some basic guidelines that will help build a small group ministry that emerges from your context and helps the congregation fulfill its mission to make disciples of Jesus Christ for the transformation of the world:

Understanding Your Role

Your task as a leader is to develop a system of small groups that emerges from and works with the congregation's context and culture. (This is rarely tidy.)

Do not try to do all this alone! If you are in a large membership church, you will probably share this responsibility with a member of the staff. If there is no staff other than the pastor, it will be all the more helpful to create a core team to work with you and the small group ministries council—as partners in this ministry. The committee on nominations may suggest team members. While the system of small groups may be vastly different among churches of different sizes, there are some basic leadership responsibilities. You and your team should expect to

- participate in the church council (you) and consult with the pastor
- coordinate ministry with the leaders of existing groups
- pray about and look for the gifts and graces in others that will identify them as potential group leaders
- provide training for others who lead small groups
- work with those leaders to cultivate within them their recognition and understanding of themselves as spiritual leaders
- work with the working groups/leaders to help them understand that their group is a place of faith formation and discipleship
- identify needed new groups, help to start new groups, and assist in the refreshment or retirement of faltering groups

The Small Group Ministries Council

Small groups require much intentional support. The danger of failing to provide leadership and support is that small groups may become inward-looking cliques with little connection to the church's mission. A small group ministries council will go a long way to prevent this from happening. If you have a staff person responsible for small group ministry, then that person leads the council. Leaders of the various classes, teams, ministry groups, and other small groups will serve as members of this council. (Some of them, as you, will also be members of the church council, whose function is different.)

If you are forming a small group ministries council for the first time, your members may not expect to have this responsibility. Your first task will be to explain and interpret to them, singly or together, what the purpose of the council is, why their presence will benefit them and the church, and what the council will do.

The task of this council is to
- provide a place of covenant for the leaders of other groups, for their continued spiritual growth, accountability, and support
- "take the temperature" of each group without going into details of anything shared by members of any group
- assess the plans, goals, and accomplishments in the faith formation system of small groups (along with the church council)
- provide a place for ongoing training in small group leadership

Convene this council at least each quarter for an hour to 90 minutes. Include prayer or another means of grace; a brief training time; and time for each council member to report briefly report on the faith formation issues of her or his group, within the bounds of confidentiality of their groups. The practice of regular reporting about each group's progress and struggles assures that the small group ministry plays a critical role in the congregation's mission of making disciples of Jesus Christ for the transformation of the world.

The work of the small group ministry council will overlap the church council in membership, but should not duplicate the work of the church council. The principle focus of the *church council* will be the plans and strategies for the church's discipleship system. The primary focus of the *small group ministry council* will be on the spiritual growth and skill building of the small group leaders, particularly as it pertains to the church's and group's plans.

Center the Small Group Ministry

Allow God to open your eyes, ears, heart, and mind to your context and the culture of the congregation. Test your ideas with a small group of trusted friends, both inside and outside the church. Pray, listen, and fast as you seek God's will for this ministry.

We strongly recommend the small group ministry core team be organized as a Covenant Discipleship group. CD groups focus on mutual accountability and support for discipleship shaped by the General Rule of Discipleship: *To witness to Jesus Christ in the world and to follow his teachings through acts of compassion, justice, worship and devotion under the guidance of the Holy Spirit.* The group writes a covenant that states how the members of the group will obey the teachings of Jesus Christ, summarized in Matthew 22:37-40 and John 13:34-35. Writing a covenant and practicing weekly accountability for discipleship provides a strong foundation for developing and sustaining small group ministry that helps the congregation live out its mission with Christ in the world. (For helps on forming and sustaining CD groups see www.gbod.org/covenantdiscipleship or Resources.)

Take an Inventory of Existing Small Groups

Create a table with three columns: Grace Groups I, Grace Groups II, and Grace Groups III (see the description of these groups above or use an organizing structure that better fits your context). Place each existing group in the column where it seems *most* appropriate. Include all the various administrative committees, ministry areas, task groups or teams, choirs, classes or study groups, self-help groups, and any other small group that meets as a part of your overall ministry. The leaders of all these groups must be invited to the small group ministry council and included in the small group ministry planning. Remember, you will likely need to do some teaching and interpretation to those leaders who do not see discipleship as necessarily part of their purpose. Help them to see that they play an important role in helping the congregation make disciples of Jesus Christ for the transformation of the world.

When you have finished, look for any holes in the small group system. You should have at least one group in each column. If the congregation lacks groups in any of the columns, then that indicates a weakness in the small group system that needs to be acknowledged and changed. Ideally, your small group system will serve the entire age span of the church. At least, begin with the groups for older youth and all adults.

Leadership

Small group ministry begins with faithful, Christ-centered leaders. The pastor plays a critical role. He or she must be actively involved in planning, implementing, supporting, and participating in small groups. Ideally, the pastor leads a small group leader accountability group; perhaps your core team. This helps the pastor with his or her own discipleship and models for laity that their pastor is a disciple who needs support and accountability just like everyone else. Finally, the pastor's participation in a small group sends the message to the congregation that this is important. Good leaders never ask followers to do anything they are not willing to do themselves.

While the pastor plays an important role, most of the leadership of small groups is provided by lay people. The primary role of appointed leadership is to share pastoral power and work in partnership with the lay leadership.

Group Leaders

Small group leaders are spiritual leaders, regardless of the specific orientation of their group. This means they habitually pray, read and study the Bible, participate in worship and the Lord's Supper, and serve in mission in the community. These holy habits are essential marks of discipleship. If the mission of small groups is to form people as disciples of Jesus Christ, then leaders must be experienced, seasoned disciples themselves who understand that they also need support and accountability.

Being identified as a "spiritual leader" may be intimidating to some leaders who have not thought of themselves that way, but it need not be. Nevertheless, others will be observing their holy habits (or lack of them) and drawing conclusions about the kind of leader they see. This does not mean that all small group leaders must suddenly become Mother Teresa or Dr. Martin Luther King, but it is an encouragement to practice the means of grace and to be aware of how their ideas, attitudes, habits, and behaviors either contribute to or work against God's kingdom.

Small group leaders are persons who are familiar with grace. They are comfortable in their own skin, acknowledge freely they do not have all the answers or need to know everything. They are good listeners who bring an atmosphere of grace with them into the meeting room. They pay attention to the people in the group and encourage everyone to participate. Group leaders extend the pastoral ministry of the congregation.

Group leaders are aware of the gifts God has given them and look for gifts in others. They try to discern where God may be calling them to use their gifts on behalf of the church, community, or world. (Remember that God's gifts serve more than the local church.)

Finally, small group leaders collaborate and cooperate with fellow leaders and the pastor(s). They work together as a team to focus on their ministries and to be clear that the group is an extension of the congregation and its mission with Christ in the world. Whether the group meets for Bible study, prayer, accountability, service in the community, or ministry within the church, the leader helps the group to maintain their attention to the stated purpose. This is important because groups can easily slip into gripe or gossip sessions or be so intent on the task that they miss the opportunity for faith formation. Good leaders will keep the group focused on its mission.

IDENTIFYING POTENTIAL LEADERS

The committee on nominations will have a primary responsibility for selecting leaders for the various ministry groups, and perhaps classes. Your team and/or council will generally focus on the leaders of new groups for some aspect of spiritual formation, self-help, weekday study, or other gathering that is not directly related to the church council.

You may come at decisions for new leadership in at least two ways: a new group is needed to meet some ministry need or new people are ready to enter into a leadership position.

You and your core team, working with the leaders of existing groups, will all cultivate relationships with many of the laity participants in those groups whom God may raise up as new leaders. You and the small group ministry council members are in a perfect place to observe the spiritual growth and gifts of these people and to name, encourage, and call forth those gifts. Many people do not realize (or admit to) the abilities they have, and it is gratifying to know that someone else recognizes their gifts and potential.

Through personal contact by telephone and face-to-face conversation, invite them to a small group leader exploratory meeting. The agenda for this meeting is to put before the potential leaders the small group ministry leadership team's vision for the congregation's small group ministry. Invite participants to ask questions and discuss how the system will take shape and how they may play a role in its development. Conclude the meeting with an invitation to fast and pray and seek the Holy Spirit's guidance in how each of them should respond to the invitation to serve as a small group leader.

Explain that serving as a small group leader means participation in a Covenant Discipleship group with other small group leaders. The reason for this is that leaders need their own group for mutual support and accountability for discipleship. The Covenant Discipleship group will help the small group leaders "watch over one another in love." They will learn from, pray for, and listen to one another. This process will provide these the sustenance these leaders need for their pastoral ministry.

In addition to the weekly CD group, leaders will also be invited to serve on the small group ministry council. They would need to be oriented to that council, with information about its purpose, when it meets, and what it is doing.

LEADERSHIP TRAINING

One of the tasks that falls to you and your core team is leadership training. You do not have to do this training yourself, but under your guidance and direction, others may be recruited, either from the congregation or elsewhere, to provide occasional training.

Your group leaders will have different skills and abilities, and the gifts needed for leading the various groups may also be different. The committee on nominations can be a partner in developing training opportunities. (The annual conference and/or district generally host training events for ministry area leaders in what that ministry is.) Your training may be more general, for example:

- Group dynamics and group relationships
- Understanding the difference between facilitating, teaching, and directing meetings
- Agenda setting, planning, and achieving timely follow-through from group members
- Dealing with and healing from conflict
- Establishing good communication
- How to deal with under- and over-participation
- Starting, nurturing, and ending groups
- Understanding the life cycle of groups and how to keep them healthy
- Establishing a group covenant, including dealing with confidentiality
- Hospitality and welcoming new members
- Understanding group culture and group norms

Other ideas and priorities will come from the group leaders themselves as they run into obstacles or new situations. As group leaders meet as a council, they may realize that others are struggling with a similar issue or problem that could be resolved or alleviated with some added training.

Forming and Organizing Small Groups

new groups may arise from a personal need, a new ministry area, or a specific task. Whatever the new group is, it should fill a needed place in your Grace Groups system. Just because something can be done does not necessarily mean that it should be done. If the church is to be the church and to do what only the church can do, all your groups should be oriented in some way to accomplishing the mission of the church to make disciples for Jesus Christ. To that end, each new group has to have a clear vision of why it is being formed, what its mission is, and how it fits into the overall mission of the church.

Becoming a Group

Any group (or the church, for that matter) has a lifespan, which has been described in the shorthand of "form, storm, and norm." People come together for some reason (form); they get to know one another and figure out the stated work of the group (storm); and then develop the stronger relationships and sense of mutual purpose that allows them to become an entity with common goals, values, and ways of working and being (norm).

THE HEALTHY GROUP LIFESPAN

A longer description focuses more on the functionality: "birth, formation, stability, decline, death." *Birth* and *formation* are essentially the same as *form* and *storm*. *Stability* may be misleading, because *vitality,* not stability, is what the group needs. Vitality allows for the group to adapt, change, look ahead, evaluate honestly what it is and what it's doing, and create. Perhaps a better way to think about *stability* is by understanding that *instability* is what leads to decline and perhaps death. Many things will destabilize a group: the presence of new members, the absence or loss of members, competing tasks, time pressures, change of leadership, change or loss of vision or purpose, change of the space, and discouragement, to name a few.

For a group to remain vital, the group leader must **always** attend to both the group's life and the group's vision. A healthy group stays in a "formation—stability" loop. When circumstances change, the whole group "regroups or re-forms"—it revisits its purpose, orients new people into the group vision and culture, reaffirms its "marching orders," maintains effective communication with each other and others outside the group as necessary, and makes intelligent adjustments to its plans and strategies. When a group slips away from this healthy way of functioning, it begins to decline.

Some signs of decline are obvious; for example, people "vote with their feet" and go elsewhere; withhold their time, money, or commitment; get cantankerous with each other; or create winners and losers by voting instead of working by consensus. Some are less obvious, but can be equally deadly: becoming too consumed with *doing* to pay attention to *being,* getting lax about maintaining the means of grace that mark the group as ministry, failing to welcome or properly orient new people, wishing for difference circumstances rather than dealing with current reality, and so on.

THE DEATH OF A GROUP

A strong leader will act to keep the group stable and vital, and may intervene at the point of decline. When the pattern of decline is not attended to, the group will eventually die, though that could take a very long time. We have all seen sad examples of a group that has dwindled in size to just a few people who most often have no real sense of mission or purpose anymore; they hang on because of their relationships.

Even at the point of death, a creative intervention may breathe new life and purpose into a faltering group, though its members may have to agree to a change that seems radical to them. Dying, however, for a "resurrection people," can be liberating and should be handled with dignity. No one need feel as if their participation and the strong relationships have all come to naught, but sometimes people don't know how to come to a graceful end. As the small group ministry leader, you may be the one who steps in to end it.

Always remember the personal touch, and never underestimate the power of ritual. If you step in, visit each of the remaining group members, one at a time, with a member of your core team, if you can. (Witnesses to this conversation are important, as feelings may run hot and deep.) Having that personal attention, in which you invite the person to reflect on what the group has been and might yet become through a rebirthing process with others, sends the appropriate message that they and the group are valued. Invite remaining group members to be mentors or advisors or "seed members" of a new group. Celebrate their life as a group in worship or with some other recognition. Find a way to keep their group "story"—their contributions to the church—alive.

Establishing a Healthy Group Culture

It is far easier in a new group to establish a culture, which we might call a rule of life, than to try to change it. Disciple-making in the Wesleyan tradition is guided by a rule of life, noted in the *Discipline*, that shapes the life and work of every group at every level of the congregation.

A RULE OF LIFE

Marjorie Thompson, writing in *Soul Feast*, describes a rule of life as "a pattern of spiritual disciplines that provides structure and direction for growth in holiness.... It fosters gifts of the Spirit in personal life and human community, helping to form us into the persons God intends us to be."

The General Rules are the United Methodist rule of life. These rules are very simple: to do no harm, to do good, and to do the works of piety. The General Rules help Christians in the Wesleyan tradition orient their corporate and individual lives toward Christ and his reign in the world. It is like a compass that helps keep a traveler on course to his or her destination, which for United Methodists is holiness of heart and life. (See "The Nature, Design, and General Rules of Our United Societies," ¶104, for a more complete description.)

ACCOUNTABILITY

Accountability in disciple-making small groups is simply sharing what you have done, or not done, as you strive to live the way of Jesus. This way of giving account is guided by the congregation's rule of life. The purpose is to support members' growth in holiness. In addition, members make commitments to the group life and group task and are expected to follow through.

Accountability is an essential practice that helps us make sure we are walking with Christ. Small group participation must include a process of mutual accountability for how members have been practicing discipleship shaped by the rule of life.

Accountability in small groups may take many forms depending upon the nature of each group. Groups may use the General Rules as the guide for shared and personal life. For example, administrative ministries (finance, trustees, staff/pastor parish relations, administrative council/board) and discipleship ministries (education, mission, evangelism, membership care, etc.) may set aside time once a quarter to evaluate their work in light of the General Rules. They may ask themselves how they have contributed to the church's mission by doing no harm, doing good, and practicing the works of piety. Such corporate accountability would serve to focus the group's work on serving Christ in the world and contributing to the congregation's mission. The key is to work together to keep Christ at the center of all they do.

The same model of accountability may apply to the more traditional small groups such as prayer, Bible study, support, nurture, cell, and accountability. These have a more explicit goal of Christian formation for their members. They may adopt the General Rules as their rule of life. They too need to decide how and how often they will take time to check themselves against their rule of life.

Groups may write a covenant that states how they will follow the General Rules. A covenant is a useful means for keeping groups focused on their mission and keeping Christ at the center. A written covenant also simplifies accountability. The group simply checks its actions and decisions against its covenant. This helps them see where their strengths and weaknesses are so they can make any needed "course corrections."

We must make clear that accountability in small groups is simply each person sharing with the group what he or she has done, or not done, guided by the congregation's rule of life or the group's covenant. The challenge is to share in ways that build up the group and help other group members with their discipleship. This practice is very important because it builds trust and intimacy within the group. As members grow closer to one another, they will also grow closer to God.

SUPPORT FOR ALL SMALL GROUP PARTICIPANTS

Small group ministry that is integral to the mission of the church requires regular, intentional support. Plan quarterly gatherings for everyone participating in a small group; not just the leaders. These gatherings will ideally include sharing a meal, a brief time of small group training, informal conversation, and worship. These gatherings are important because they will build connections between all the various groups and provide ongoing training. They are an opportunity for groups to learn from one another.

Quarterly gatherings are ideally for small group participants only. They are not open to everyone in the congregation. Members of the congregation who wish to participate in the quarterly meetings may do so on the condition they join one of the small groups.

Finally, the recommended order of worship for the conclusion of the meeting is the Love Feast found in *The United Methodist Book of Worship* on page 581. The Love Feast is an important part of Methodist spirituality. It is a powerful time of informal worship that includes hymn singing, Scripture reading, prayer, testimony, sharing bread and water, and receiving a collection for the poor. One of its important features is that it is intended to be led entirely by lay women and men. The love feast empowers laity and builds community among persons who share the common experience of participation in a small group.

Evaluation

regular evaluation is crucial for excellence and faithfulness in any ministry. But what do we evaluate? How do we know when we have the results we want? If the ultimate goal is making disciples for Jesus Christ, how do we recognize a "disciple"?

Goals

There is not much point in evaluating if you don't know what you want to accomplish or if there has been no goal setting. Start with the mission or purpose of the group. If it is a Bible study group, a probable result is that you want group members who are biblically literate and have some understanding of how to apply those texts to life.

So, envision what a successful and faithful result will be, given the purpose of the group, and then set three or four strategies or goals that will help you get there. Goal setting begins with the stated mission or purpose of the group. Goals should be SMART—specific, measurable, attainable, reasonable, and timely. Goals should be specific; challenging, but not impossible; and doable over a designated short- and long-term. Accomplishing short-term goals encourages group members to keep going, and long-term goals help keep the group member's eyes on the "main thing." One easy question for your core team and each small group to consider is this: "If we continue on our current trajectory—keeping the same attitudes, ideas, plans, and activities without change—will we be likely to achieve the results we want?" If you're not so sure the answer is yes, reexamine and rework your current direction.

To return to the example above, goals for that Bible study group might include teaching how to navigate the Scriptures; introducing the major themes and key biblical figures; and issuing a weekly challenge to group members that relates to a person, theme, or biblical value. Once those goals or strategies are set, you can measure the results. Remember—if you are not getting the results you want, change your goals and strategies.

Measurement

There are two fundamental measurement criteria used to evaluate any process, project, or performance: *quantitative* and *qualitative*. *Quantitative* metrics measure in numbers and amounts. For example, a worship service achieves an attendance goal of exceeding 100 worshippers weekly, a children's Vacation Bible School sets a goal of 50 children a day, or a church sets a membership goal of five new members a month. Quantitative measures are easy—just count. *Qualitative* measures are a bit more difficult. Following the earlier examples, how well did worship connect the 100 people to a sense of God's holiness? What did the 50 children learn about God, faith, and their Christian behavior each day they attended VBS? How well do the five new members this month grow in their discipleship, and how are they living their faith in the world? These are qualitative measures.

Measurement of small groups begins with missional counting. We begin with the obvious:

- How many small groups that fit the definition cited in the introduction are currently active?
- How many people are participating in small groups?
- What percentage of the congregation's membership is participating in at least one small group?
- What is the percentage change (increase or decrease) of small group participation from the previous year?

We can combine quantitative and qualitative measurement. Another way to think about *metrics* is to identify the *standards* that illustrate faithful and effective discipleship. This helps remind us of the results we want through small group ministries and how we know we have achieved them, for example:

- How many small group participants are serving as a leader in discipleship for the first time this year?
- How many members served in mission in the community (i.e., served at a soup kitchen, visited the sick, visited in jail or prison, helped build homes for low income families, visited the homebound, and so on)?
- How many members are serving in worship leadership for the first time (reading Scripture, serving as an usher, singing in choir, playing a musical instrument, serving Holy Communion, etc.)?
- How many people are certified lay servants for the first time? How many have completed advanced lay servant training?
- How many members are habitually practicing the means of grace through weekly worship, daily prayer (private and with friends/family), the Lord's Supper, Bible reading and study, fasting or abstinence, or engaging in a service or justice ministry?
- How do the personal stories of the participants reveal that lives are being changed and becoming more like the image of Christ?
- How are those stories confirmed in the community of faith?

It is never enough to determine the success or failure of small group ministries in terms of the number of small groups, the number of people involved, how often they meet, or how many new groups get launched. Beyond these standards and measures, it is important to understand how people's lives are being changed and how they are growing in holiness of heart and life. Remember, a group of 10 people who reorient their lives to be full-time disciples is much more impressive than 500 people who sit in circles in small groups talking about what fun activities they would like to do together.

One simple, periodic process to follow is to answer the following questions with the whole leadership of the congregation:

1. What is our mission and purpose as a congregation?
2. What roles do small groups play in helping us fulfill our mission and reach our goals as a congregation?
3. What do we want small groups to provide for participants?
4. How well are our existing small groups meeting these needs?
5. How can we improve existing groups to offer more to participants?
6. What other groups could we offer to enable more people to grow in holiness of heart and life and to help this congregation fulfill its mission?

These questions cannot be answered quantitatively. Assessing the role of small groups in spiritual formation and helping the congregation fulfill its mission are only possible when we include qualitative metrics in our evaluation. By establishing the standards that you want to live up to and grow toward, and which you evaluate regularly, you have a strong base on which to build your ministries, groups, and members. For more helps on measurement, planning, and evaluation, see the Guide to the Guidelines on the CD and visit www.umvitalcongregations.com.

Conclusion

discipleship is a process of growth in faith, hope, and love. It is a way of living that draws us closer to Christ and conforms our lives to his. A helpful way of visualizing this life comes from a Sixth Century monk, Dorotheos of Gaza. He describes the Christian life with the following illustration of a circle with lines radiating inward to a central point.

> Suppose we were to take a compass and insert the point and draw the outline of a circle. The center point is the same distance from any point on the circumference.... Let us suppose that this circle is the world and that God himself is the center: the straight lines drawn from the circumference to the center are the lives of human beings.... Let us assume for the sake of analogy that to move toward God, then, human beings move from the circumference along the various radii of the circle to the center. But at the same time, the closer they are to God, the closer they become to one another; and the closer they are to one another, the closer they become to God.

(From *To Love as God Loves: Conversations with the Early Church*, by Roberta C. Bondi)

Discipleship is how we move from the circumference of the circle closer and closer to the center. In the process we grow in holiness of heart and life and are drawn closer and closer to our neighbor and to God. Living the General Rules within relationships of mutual accountability and support in small groups empowers and equips women, men, youth and children to grow up and grow toward the One who is creating, redeeming, and sustaining them in love. Providing the means for adults, youth and children to live out the Baptismal Covenant and grow in holiness of heart and life requires a system of small groups. Regardless of size, location, or ethnicity, small groups are the most effective means of inviting people into a relationship with Jesus Christ and equipping them to grow in holiness of heart and life.

Resources

**Indicates our top picks

SMALL GROUP MINISTRY

**Biblical Foundations for Small Group Ministry: An Integrational Approach*, by Gareth Weldon Icenogle (Downers Grove: InterVarsity Press, 1994. ISBN 0-8308-1771-9).

Building a Church of Small Groups: A Place Where Nobody Stands Alone, by Bill Donahue & Russ Robinson (Grand Rapids: Zondervan, 2005. ISBN 978-0-310-26710-2).

**Class Leaders: Recovering a Tradition*, by David Lowes Watson (Eugene: Wipf & Stock Publishers, 2002. ISBN 978-1-57910-954-7).

**Community That Is Christian: A Handbook on Small Groups*, by Julie A. Gorman (Grand Rapids: Baker Books, 1993, 2002. ISBN 0-8010-9145-4).

**Covenant Discipleship: Christian Formation Through Mutual Accountability*, by David Lowes Watson (Eugene: Wipf & Stock Publishers, 2002. ISBN 978-1-57910-953-0).

**Forming Christian Disciples: The Role of Covenant Discipleship and Class Leaders in the Congregation*, by David Lowes Watson (Eugene: Wipf & Stock Publishers, 2002. ISBN 978-1-57910-946-2).

Making Small Groups Work: What Every Small Group Leader Needs to Know, by Henry Cloud & John Townsend (Grand Rapids: Zondervan, 2010. ISBN 0-310-25028-5).

**Missional Small Groups: Becoming a Community That Makes a Difference in the World*, by M. Scott Boren (Grand Rapids: Baker Books, 2010. ISBN 978-0-8010-7230-7).

The Relational Way: From Small Group Structures to Holistic Life Connections, by M. Scott Boren (Houston: TOUCH Publications, 2007. ISBN 0-978-8779-0-X).

BIBLICAL AND THEOLOGICAL FOUNDATIONS

**Accountable Discipleship: Living in God's Household*, by Steven W. Manskar (Nashville: Discipleship Resources, 2000. ISBN 978-0-881-77-339-2).

**Blueprint for Discipleship: Wesley's General Rules as a Guide for Christian Living*, by Kevin M. Watson (Nashville: Discipleship Resources, 2009. ISBN 978-0-88177-556-3).

The Early Methodist Class Meeting: Its Origins and Significance, by David Lowes Watson (Eugene: Wipf & Stock Publishers, 2002. ISBN 978-1-57910-939-4).

**The Forgotten Ways: Reactivating the Missional Church*, by Alan Hirsch (Grand Rapids: Brazos Press, 2006. ISBN 978-1-58743-164-7).

The Forgotten Ways Handbook: A Practical Guide for Developing Missional Churches, by Alan Hirsch & Darryn Altclass (Grand Rapids: Brazos Press, 2009. ISBN 978-1-58743-249-1).

Grace to Lead: Practicing Leadership in The Wesleyan Tradition, by Kenneth L. Carder and Laceye C. Warner (Nashville: General Board of Higher Education and Ministry, 2010. ISBN 978-0-938162-76-6).

Reclaiming the Wesleyan Tradition: John Wesley's Sermons for Today, by Douglas M. Strong et al. (Nashville: Discipleship Resources, 2007. ISBN 978-0-88177-519-8).

CD WITH STUDY GUIDE
**"Opening Ourselves to Grace: Basic Christian Practices" (Nashville: Discipleship Resources, 2007. ISBN 978-0-88177-508-2).

WEBSITES
GBOD Small Group Ministry Resources
http://www.gbod.org/smallgroups

http://www.gbod.org/covenantdiscipleship

The Upper Room—Small Groups
http://www.upperroom.org/fivecircles/walking.asp